UNSTOPPABLE

Become unstoppable in 30 minutes or less

FRANCIS JONAH

IMPORTANT

My name is Francis Jonah. I believe all things are possible. It is because of this belief that I have achieved so much in life. This belief extends to all. I believe every human being is equipped to succeed in every circumstance, regardless of the circumstance.

I know the only gap that exists between you and what you need to achieve or overcome is knowledge.

People are destroyed for lack of knowledge.

It is for this reason that I write short practical books that are so simple, people begin to experience immediate results as evidenced by the many testimonies I receive on a daily basis for my various books.

This book is no exception. You will obtain results because of it.

Visit my website for powerful articles and materials

www.francisjonah.com

FREE GIFT

Just to say Thank You for downloading my book, I'd like to give you these books for free.

Download these 4 powerful books today for free and give yourself a great future.

Click Here to Download

Your testimonies will abound. Click Here to see my other books. They have produced many testimonies and I want your testimony to be one too.

Counselling Or Prayer

Send me an email if you need prayer or counsel or you have a question.

Better still if you want to make my acquaintance

My email is drfrancisjonah@gmail.com

Other books by Francis Jonah

1. 3 Day Fasting Challenge: How to receive manifestation of answers

2. How to Have Outrageous Financial Abundance In No Time:Biblical Principles For Immediate And Overwhelming Financial Success

3. 5 Bible Promises, Prayers and Decrees That Will Give You The Best Year Ever: A book for Shaping Every Year Successfully plus devotional (Book Of Promises 1)

4. Influencing The Unseen Realm: How to Influence The Spirit Realm for Victory in The Physical Realm(Spiritual Success Books)

5. [Prayer That Works: Taking Responsibility For Answered Prayer](#)

6. [Healing The Sick In Five Minutes:How Anyone Can Heal Any Sickness](#)

7. [The Financial Miracle Prayer](#)

8. [The Best Secret To Answered Prayer](#)

9. [The Believer's Authority(Authority Of The Believer,Power And Authority Of The Believer)](#)

10. [The Healing Miracle Prayer](#)

11. I Shall Not Die: Secrets To Long Life And Overcoming The Fear of Death

12. Three Straightforward Steps To Outrageous Financial Abundance: Personal Finance (Finance Made Easy Book 1)

13. Prayers For Financial Miracles: And 3 Ways To Receive Answers Quickly

14. Book: 3 Point Blueprint For Building Strong Faith: Spiritual:Religious:Christian:Motivational

15. How To Stop Sinning Effortlessly

16. The Power Of Faith-Filled Words

17. All Sin Is Paid For: An Eye Opening Book

18. Be Happy Now:No More Depression

19. The Ultimate Christian: How To Win In Every Life Situation: A book full of Revelations

20. Books:How To Be Free From Sicknesses And Diseases(Divine Health): Divine Health Scriptures

21. Multiply Your Personal Income In Less Than 30 Days

22. Ultimate Method To Memorize The Bible Quickly: (How To Learn Scripture Memorization)

23. Overcoming Emotional Abuse

24. Passing Exams The Easy Way: 90% and above in exams (Learning Simplified)

25. Books:Goal Setting For Those In A Hurry To Achieve Fast

26. Do Something Lest You Do Nothing

27. Financial Freedom:My Personal Blue-Print Made Easy For Men And Women

28. Why Men Go To Hell

29. Budgeting Tools And How My Budget Makes Me More Money

30. How To Raise Capital In 72 Hours: Quickly and Effectively Raise Capital Easily in Unconventional Ways (Finance Made Easy)

31. How To Love Unconditionally

32. Financial Independence: The Simple Path I Used To Wealth

33. Finding Happiness: The Story Of John Miller: A Christian Fiction

34. Finance Made Easy (2 Book Series)

Click here to see my author page

TABLE OF CONTENT

INTRODUCTION 15

CHAPTER ONE 18

CHAPTER TWO 22

CHAPTER THREE 25

CHAPTER FOUR 29

CHAPTER FIVE 32

CHAPTER SIX 36

CHAPTER SEVEN 41

CHAPTER EIGHT 47

CHAPTER NINE 52

CHAPTER TEN 57

CHAPTER ELEVEN 62

CHAPTER TWELVE 67

CHAPTER THIRTEEN 72

INTRODUCTION

Who art thou, O great mountain? before Zerubbabel thou shalt become a plain

Zechariah 4:7a

When a group of engineers were given the task of building a road through a huge mountain, they were more than perplexed, they were dejected.

This was an impossible task and everyone shared the same sentiment.

Nonetheless, their employer asked them to deliver exactly that. Deliver the impossible task.

A few years later, the engineers had built a road through the mountain. They had done what was impossible.

You are unstoppable.

There is no task or assignment or challenge before you that you cannot overcome.

That is your design.

You were designed in such a way that nothing should be able to stop you in life.

What is that thing you need to achieve?

What is the goal you need to accomplish?

What is the challenge you need to overcome?

What is that mountain in front of you right now?

Is it to achieve a certain result in school?

Is it to raise an amount of money?

Is it to rise up from your sick bed or to heal one who is sick?

Is it to raise the dead or break a cycle of setback and disappointment?

Fear not, you are unstoppable. It is not beyond you.

This is the starting point for your achievement.

Know that you are unstoppable. This knowledge coupled with the revelations in this book will catapult you and everyone around you to levels beyond comprehension.

> **Eze 2:2 And the spirit entered into me when he spake unto me, and set me upon my feet, that I heard him that spake unto me.**
>
> **Ezekiel 2:2**

The words that will enter into you will cause mighty breakthroughs and break massive barriers.

CHAPTER ONE

KEEP KNOCKING

Mat 7:8 For every one that asketh receiveth; and he that seeketh findeth; and to him that knocketh it shall be opened.

Matthew 7:8

Have you ever had a knock on your door that you ignored?

There was a man who ignored the knock of a woman seeking help. The woman kept knocking regardless of the fact that she was being ignored.

The man was a judge who could help her. He had what it took to help her.

The woman knew he was at home so she kept knocking. The judge being tired of her knocking opened the door and offered her what she wanted so that she could leave him alone.

This is a lesson everyone needs to understand. Too many people give up too early on wonderful door and opportunities just because the first knock did not have any response. A young man decided to start his own business. He kept asking for partners to help him start the business. The more he asked, the more he was rejected. Well, he did not stop asking; he kept on improving his proposal and business plan every time he was rejected.

Finally the business plan and proposal became so irresistible, he had more partners than he needed.

Success comes to the man who keeps moving, who keeps improving, who keeps overcoming obstacles.

The man who gives up easily would never know what would have been of that opportunity or that relationship.

There is a reason quitters never win and winners never quit.

It is not only about not quitting, it is about improving and keeping at it.

It is only an unwise man that does the same thing and expects different results.

He who plants oranges and expects a harvest of apples will never have his expectations met in a thousand years.

There must be improvement, there must be changes to increase your chances of getting a different result.

The little improvements go a long way to take you to your next level.

Keep knocking and perhaps let the latter knock be louder than the former.

When you knock, the door must be opened.

Yes, it must be opened. It is the law of God. It is the law of the universe.

Keep pressing for it is said, where there is a will, there is a way.

As long as you keep pressing, you will make a way where there seemed to be no way.

CHAPTER TWO

IT IS NOTHING, YET IT IS EVERYTHING

Pro 18:16 A man's gift maketh room for him, and bringeth him before great men.

Proverbs 18:16

The number of people who look down on their gifts and talents is shocking.

I saw a lady who had such a great voice and the ability to effortlessly put down lyrics.

On the few occasions I saw her sing, I was marvelled. Such greatness in one vessel and yet she did not appreciate this great gift she had.

She actually did little with her singing and writing.

It was so easy for her to do these two things that she took them for granted.

Therein lies the failure of many people. The gifts and talents that God has given to them have been underestimated. Some have even despised their gifts.

The fact that you can do something easily does not mean it is easy for everyone.

Recognise what you have and maximize it.

Don't die with that ability.

Don't take the books you can write to the grave.

Don't take your gift of encouragement away.

Don't take your inventions to the grave.

Don't take your instrument playing ability to the grave.

Don't take your business to the grave.

Don't take your brainstorming gift to the grave.

Don't take your teaching gift to the grave.

Rather, identify that thing which you love and do effortlessly. Polish it. Develop it.

If it is raw, people would not appreciate it as they should.

Find ways of making it better. Get guidance. Get mentorship but at all cost polish the gift.

Thereafter present it to the world and keep packaging it and presenting it till it makes a difference.

That gift must and will set you apart.

Say it to yourself. "My gift must and will set me apart".

Put it to work, do not relax and you will go places with your God-given gift.

CHAPTER THREE

POWER PRODUCING FACTORY

The effectual fervent prayer of a righteous man availeth much.

James 5:16b

You are born again.

You are a wonder to your generation.

You are a power producing factory.

You can produce and release power at will. Glory to God.

Why are you downcast when you have the ability to release power that is dynamic in its working.

Men ought to pray always because in prayer, tremendous power is released.

Power that deals with self as well as circumstances.

Power that heals the sick.

Power that raises the dead.

Power that causes rain to fall.

Power that cause the blind to see.

Power that brings increase.

Power that brings favour.

Power that calms the storms.

Power that shuts the mouth of lions.

That power is resident in you.

Your prayer grabs circumstances and brings them to its will.

That power cannot be stopped as long as your mouth is opened in heartfelt prayer.

See it released right now as you open your mouth.

It must be heartfelt.

It must be continuous and once it is, understand that power to produce results will be released.

That is how Elijah produced rain.

That is how Jesus produced mighty results.

That is the way of power.

Stay in prayer and come out as a mighty man of power and results.

    1. To cure prayerlessness, an inconsistent prayer life and the pain of not enjoying all that God has made available to you,, click [here](#) to learn more about my [3 Day Course](#) on "How to Overcome prayerlessness" that will solve the problem of prayerlessness in your life.

    2. To overcome the pain of not having enough money to live where you want, eat what you want to eat and be a blessing to the multitudes around

you, I have created a [7 Day Financial Abundance Course](#) that will deliver financial abundance to you quickly.

Click [here](#) to learn more about that course.

You will see increase and enlargement as you step out in faith.

CHAPTER FOUR

REALITY PRODUCTION LINE

Eph 3:20 Now unto him that is able to do exceeding abundantly above all that we ask or think, according to the power that worketh in us,

Ephesians 3:20

The mind is a production line. If you can see it in your mind, you give God the template to bring it into reality.

Men have brought evil upon themselves with their minds but we cease to be in the class of such men.

Abraham was told that what he saw was what he was going to get.

That is the power of the mind in use.

Your mind is powerful. It is up to you to create the pictures of the life you want in it and you can be sure that it will be produced picture perfect for you.

This was the same formula Jacob implemented when he put an image in the minds of his sheep for them to produce the exact image of what he had placed into their minds.

Gen 30:38 And he set the rods which he had pilled before the flocks in the gutters in the watering troughs when the flocks came to drink, that they should conceive when they came to drink.

Gen 30:39 And the flocks conceived before the rods, and brought forth cattle ringstraked, speckled, and spotted.

Genesis 30:38-39

You have a powerful mind that can roam independent of circumstances. Release from your present circumstances and let it create the future you are looking for.

Speak the image you want into your mind. Your mind will capture the picture. Hold on to this image till it manifests in the realm of the physical.

The imagination is a powerful tool that God has blessed you with.

Use it and use it well for that is how the tower of Babel which was destined to reach heaven was built.

It was conceived in the imagination and only God could stop it once it had gotten to the place of the imagination.

Yes, you also have the all important tool of the imagination.

Use it to your benefit.

CHAPTER FIVE

UNITY

Mat 18:19 Again I say unto you, That if two of you shall agree on earth as touching any thing that they shall ask, it shall be done for them of my Father which is in heaven.

Matthew 18:19

Jesus worked in unity with twelve disciples. With that united front, he was able to achieve much.

Even when he died, his disciples and others he united with continued the work.

What you cannot do alone, you can do with another. Collaboration is something that must be taught more because many people want to go solo when they can do much in collaboration with others.

The Bible clearly tells us that if two collaborate and agree on anything, it shall be done of them of God in heaven.
this tells us how much God loves it when we unite with the brethren.

Satan hates the unity of the brethren, that is why he authors confusion.

He knows what can be accomplished when people are one.

You will recall that apart from imagining the tower of Babel, the people were united. They were one.

This helped them greatly in progressing the agenda they had.

There are many things you can do faster and better if you would just find someone or people to unite with.

It is true you can do it alone but understand that we have just one life.

We need to make the best out of it. That includes taking advantage of every little opportunity we have.

Looking for opportunities of collaboration will bless you greatly.

It will make you unstoppable.

One shall indeed chase a thousand but two shall chase ten thousand:

Deu 32:30 How should one chase a thousand, and two put ten thousand to flight, except their Rock had sold them, and the LORD had shut them up?

Deuteronomy 32:30

There is so much power and momentum in unity. You are being stopped because you are doing things alone.

Determine that from today you will unite with someone or people and you will release the inherent power that resides in unity.

Unity is strength indeed.

CHAPTER SIX

WORDS

Words are the means of transportation from the spirit realm to the realm of the physical.

Whatever you are saying is an act of transportation to the physical realm.

This is why your negative words will bring negative impact and your positive words will bring positive impact in your life.

This is why the Bible says death and life are in our tongues. Not only that, the Bible says we shall eat the fruit of our tongue:

Pro 18:21 Death and life are in the power of the tongue: and they that love it shall eat the fruit thereof.

Proverbs 18:21

Whatever you are enjoying in your life is as a result of your tongue. What you are enjoying today, you said it yesterday.

What you will enjoy today is what you are saying today.

You are only transporting things into your life with your words.

Find that man or woman who wants to change his life. His words must be an indication of what he wants to see in his life.

Pain, sorrow, death, defeat and poverty can be transported by the tongue.

In the same way, blessings, wealth, health and joy can be transported by words.

God the Almighty created the whole world with His words.

This is testament of the power of words.

Brethren it is time we start speaking right.

Speak right to your children. Speak right to your workers. Speak right to your spouse. Speak right to the people around you.

Your words will build them up.

That child who is behaving stubbornly must be changed with the power of words.

It is better to call that child great man than to emphasize the stubbornness.

It is better to call yourself rich than to emphasize your poverty.

The just live by faith.

They do not say what they see physically. They speak what they believe.

They say I am rich.

This will transport riches from the spirit realm to them.

The poor man who keeps saying I am poor will never break free from the cycle of poverty.

He will have what he says.

Jesus rightly put it in the book of Mark:

> *Mar 11:23 For verily I say unto you, That whosoever shall say unto this mountain, Be thou removed, and be thou cast into the sea; and shall not doubt in his heart, but shall believe that those things which he saith shall come to pass; he shall have whatsoever he saith.*
>
> *Mark 11:23*

He shall have whatever he says. That was the emphasis of the statement.

There could be a waiting time, there could be hindrances, but the truth is that, what you are going to have is what you say.

It is better you speak right than to speak wrong.

Beloved, there is power in your words. Explore it to the maximum.

You are not helpless. You have words that can uplift you from discouragement and depression.

Words that can lift you from pain and sorrow.

Use them. Use them, for there is life in them.

CHAPTER SEVEN

HUNGER

Hunger is one of the drivers of greatness in this world.

When you are satisfied, you can never be filled again.

> *Mat 5:6 Blessed are they which do hunger and thirst after righteousness: for they shall be filled.*
>
> *Matthew 5:6*

When you hunger and thirst, what automatically follows is a filling.

Hunger is thus a prerequisite for receiving filling.

What are you looking to be filled with? Is your hunger for it great enough?

One of the things that must be developed in your life to make you unstoppable is hunger.

Too many people have lost their hunger in life.

They have lost their hunger for God.

They have lost their hunger for excellence.

They have lost their hunger for prosperity.

They have lost their hunger for ministry.

They have lost their hunger for success.

That is the root of the problem.

When you lose your hunger, you lose your appetite to pursue and achieve.

This is an attack of the enemy and once he succeeds in discouraging you and causing you to lose your hunger, he does not have to do more.

This is why you must feed your hunger.

The man that read of another winning 100 souls for God had his hunger stirred up and immediately began on a quest to win more souls for God.

He surpassed what he read but that reading was the catalyst to stirring up his hunger.

The man that sat in the vehicle of his co-worker was stirred to know that there was something better available for him. His exposure to that vehicle stirred up his hunger.

He knew he had to change his car. His hunger was stirred. Needless to say, that hunger led him to get a better car for himself.

Pray that your hunger would be restored because it is a critical element that will propel you to pursue.

Not only will you pursue, you will overtake.

Such is the way of hunger.

It keeps you awake at night.

It compels you to go the extra mile.

It harasses you till you do what you must do.

They that hunger are filled. They that thirst are filled.

You may be hungry but is that hunger stronger than your laziness, is your hunger stronger than your tiredness, is your hunger stronger than all the 75 excuses your mind keeps giving to you?

I know of a man who watched others pray for hours and his hunger for prayer was also stirred.

Do whatever it takes to stir up your hunger for success.

There is no obstacle you cannot surmount. The important thing is that you are hungry enough to rise and take steps forward.

Hunger is a great driver.

Build it in you and you can achieve anything at all in this world.

Remember that the hungry will be filled. The hungry will pursue. The hungry will identify what they need and go for it.

Are you hungry enough? If not, work on that hunger today and the rest will fall in place.

My desire is to see your progress and prosperity and freedom from negative people and circumstances. Because of that, please permit me to introduce two courses that I believe passionately will help you.

1. To cure prayerlessness, an inconsistent prayer life and the pain of not enjoying all that God has made available to you,, click here to learn more about my 3 Day Course on "How to Overcome prayerlessness" that will solve the problem of prayerlessness in your life.

2.To overcome the pain of not having enough money to live where you want, eat what you want to eat and be a blessing to the multitudes around you, I have created a *7 Day Financial Abundance Course* that will deliver financial abundance to you quickly.

Click here to learn more about that course.

You will see increase and enlargement as you step out in faith.

CHAPTER EIGHT

REPRESENTING GOD

Among all his creations, God chose man to represent Him fully here on earth.

Concerning the believer, He said:

Rom 5:17 For if by one man's offence death reigned by one; much more they which receive abundance of grace and of the gift of righteousness shall reign in life by one, Jesus Christ.)

Romans 5:17

We are supposed to reign in life by one, Jesus Christ.

Ours is the place of Kings. God is the King of Kings because we are Kings and He is our King.

Everything Jesus went through was to bring us to the point of reigning in life.

It was to bring us to the point of bringing to pass the heart desires of God here on earth.

We are to dominate over the devil and bring men and women to the saving knowledge of Christ.

God has so much trust in us that He has made us His co-workers.

We carry out His works on earth but ultimately He works in us:

2Co 6:1 We then, as workers together with him, beseech you also that ye receive not the grace of God in vain.

2 Corinthians 6:1

We are workers together with God. We have a mission of representing Him fully on earth.

We are to bring his power, his love, his forgiveness to humankind.

This is why He wants you to heal the sick, raise the dead, cast out devils and even cleanse lepers.

It is high time you stepped into your purpose.

This is not the time to be small. This is the time to humble yourself under the eternal purposes of God and take your place in this life.

Remember:

Psa 82:6 I have said, Ye are gods; and all of you are children of the most High.

Psa 82:7 But ye shall die like men, and fall like one of the princes.

The children of God must rise and show the nature of God in them.

You must rise and show that you are a partaker of divine nature. Greater is He that is in you than He that is in the world.

God is gracious.

There is nothing in this world bigger than you. The greater one is in you.

He is greater than your worries, than your bills, than your burdens.

He lives in you and you represent Him.

What cannot defeat Him cannot defeat you.

What cannot bring Him down cannot bring you down.

What cannot silence Him cannot silence you.

You represent Him.

No wonder He said:

Mat 18:18 Verily I say unto you, Whatsoever ye shall bind on earth shall be bound in heaven: and whatsoever ye shall loose on earth shall be loosed in heaven.

Matthew 18:18

Such power has been given to men like you. Don't just stand there in awe. Meditate on it. Let this truth rise within you and take your position as the representative of God.

He calls you an ambassador:

> ***2Co 5:20 Now then we are ambassadors for Christ, as though God did beseech you by us: we pray you in Christ's stead, be ye reconciled to God.***
>
> ***2 Corinthians 5:20***

You are hereby reminded of your commission to represent heaven as an ambassador on earth.

Go you. There is so much hope and believe in you that you will do well.

CHAPTER NINE

DEAD TO SIN

When man fell, he fell from glory and became a servant of sin:

> *Rom 3:23 For all have sinned, and come short of the glory of God;*
>
> *Romans 3:23*

The story did not end there. Jesus Christ came in to intervene on behalf of man.

This intervention did so many things for man including making him dead to sin and giving a new nature.

This nature given to him was the very nature of God.

> *2Co 5:17 Therefore if any man be in Christ, he is a new creature: old things are passed away; behold, all things are become new.*

2 Corinthians 5:17

God did a beautiful thing for man to help him overcome sin on a daily basis. He made man dead to sin:

> *Rom 6:2 God forbid. How shall we, that are dead to sin, live any longer therein?*
>
> *Romans 6:2*

This means that the believer is free from the jurisdiction and power of sin and can live above the rule of sin.

Hitherto, the power of sin held man bound like a slave, but thanks to Jesus, every believer has been freed from the power of sin and is free to live a righteous life.

We are not dying to sin.

We are dead to sin.

It means this very day the power and hold of sin has been broken over our lives.

God has delivered you from the power of sin.

Do not re-submit yourself to it.

The devil is ready to ruin you if you do:

Rom 6:16 Know ye not, that to whom ye yield yourselves servants to obey, his servants ye are to whom ye obey; whether of sin unto death, or of obedience unto righteousness?

Romans 6:16

Resist the temptation to yield yourself to the devil and sin.

You have been freed from them.

What you could not do on your own has been done for you.

Victory has been delivered to you. Hold on to it.

Fight that battle every day to hold on to the victory that has been delivered to you.

Resist every temptation, resist every evil desire.

I will not be bound by something I am free from.

I will not submit to something that has lost power over me.

I will not yield to an inferior force that seeks to destroy me.

Psa 119:9 BETH. Wherewithal shall a young man cleanse his way? by taking heed thereto according to thy word.

Psalm 119: 9

Your key is to listen to and do the word.

The devil is out there looking for a victim and you will not be that victim.

Purge my soul O lord of every evil desire.

That should be your prayer as you submit your body on the altar of fire.

There is still a clarion call to all believers:

Rom 12:1 I beseech you therefore, brethren, by the mercies of God, that ye present your bodies a living sacrifice, holy, acceptable unto God, which is your reasonable service.

Romans 12:1

This is the way of victory. This is the way of glory.

This is the way of dominion.

Beloved, I thank God that you are dead to sin and alive to righteousness.

You will reign in life starting from today.

CHAPTER TEN

EXTRA MILE

Many people need a reintroduction to the person God has made them.

The believer is a special being.

The believer was created in Christ Jesus unto good works.

He is to be a light and an example to His world:

> ***Eph 2:10 For we are his workmanship, created in Christ Jesus unto good works, which God hath before ordained that we should walk in them.***
>
> ***Ephesians 2:10***

There is a particular command that Jesus gives to believers to walk in.

This is to go the extra mile in all they do.

They are not to shirk responsibility.

They are to embrace responsibility and take it to the next level.

They are supposed to do what they are given to do so well that, people will marvel at their results:

Mat 5:41 And whosoever shall compel thee to go a mile, go with him twain.

Matthew 5:41

Go the extra mile with the one that asks you to go just one mile.

Do more than is required.

That is how men make progress in this world.

Give more than is required.

That is how men ascend.

This is the very nature of God. He does more than expected:

Eph 3:20 Now unto him that is able to do exceeding abundantly above all that we ask or think, according to the power that worketh in us,

Ephesians 3:20

I choose to be a man who will not shirk responsibility.

Like Jonah, it is time to repent and take upon the responsibilities of your life.

Take up the responsibility of that child, of that department, of that office.

Do the work others will not do.

A man once lived who was given the work of another on leave.

He did this work and exceeded expectations so much that when the original man in charge of the work came, there was a dilemma on who to assign the job to.

This is the kind of dilemma you are to create in your life and ministry.

Among God's children, can you do his work so well that he will find it hard to replace you.

In that work place, in that church, in that group, can you work so hard that you are irreplaceable?

How have we fallen from our ability to do great exploits.

The spirit of excellence is upon your life.

It was on Daniel. It was on Shadrach, Meshach and Abednego. This is what made them do great things in a foreign land.

You are summoned to do more than required.

You are summoned to bring greatness to the place of your calling and duty.

You are called for the extra ordinary.

Go the extra mile.

Do more.

It is not a suggestion. It is a duty that pulls your heart.

It is the heart and desire of God for you.

CHAPTER ELEVEN

COUNT IT ALL JOY

I hated challenges.

I hated trials.

I hated temptations.

I hated difficulties.

This was all before I encountered some particular scriptures in the Bible:

> *Jas 1:2 My brethren, count it all joy when ye fall into divers temptations;*
>
> *Jas 1:3 Knowing this, that the trying of your faith worketh patience.*
>
> *Jas 1:4 But let patience have her perfect work, that ye may be perfect and entire, wanting nothing.*
>
> **James 1:2-4**

I was to count it joy when I fell into temptation.

I was to celebrate the very fact of being in a challenge.

It was a trying of my faith and it had a purpose. To work patience in me and also afford me the opportunity to grow.

Finally, it was to bring me to a place where I would want nothing.

There is no testimony without a test.

There is no victory without a battle and there is no promotion without a challenge.

Think of it. When you went to school, you had to write an exam and pass it before you could move to your next level.

Without that exam, there was no movement.

Anyone that desires movement, promotion and increase must strongly desire challenges.

Without these challenges, there is no victory on the horizon.

The current challenge you are going through will build you up.

It will cause you to learn.

It will cause you to pray.

It will take the slumber of your eyelids and the sleep of your eyes.

It will cause you to summon all your strength to press and obtain victory.

Such is the way of trials.

Such is the way of challenges.

They are designed to bring out the best in you.

There is so much potential and strength and ability within you.

Something must draw it out.

Throughout the ages, challenges have been found to do just that for any individual at all.

They press the right buttons for the right stuff to come out of a person that would lead him or her to the next level.

Change the way you are looking at your challenge.

It is not there to harm you, it is there to make you better.

It is not there to break you, it is there to make you.

Some men were gifted a powerful prayer life because of their challenges.

Some men discovered great businesses because of their challenges.

Some men stumbled upon the power of fasting because of their challenges.

No challenge is greater than you. The greater one is in you.

Can you put the challenge aside, put on some loud music and begin to celebrate.

Then after celebrating, look at that challenge in the face and make sure you deal with it once and for all.

CHAPTER TWELVE

MORE SOLUTIONS THAN PROBLEMS

I have been told and found to be true that there are indeed more solutions than problems in this world.

The tree whose active ingredient cures malaria was on this earth long before there was a disease called malaria.

The same truth applies to all other diseases. Their cures were on earth before the diseases ever existed.

Someone once said, there are several ways to kill a cat. If the cat is the problem, then it means the solution to killing this cat are many.

The same applies to your current problem. They have more solutions than you can ever come up with in a million years.

Do not become like the man who implemented two solutions and gave up on ever solving this problem.

The very fact that he found two solutions to implement gives credence to the truth that there are more solutions than problems.

The problem you face, has been faced by countless others before you. Some solved it, some ignored it and others virtually run away from it.

Solomon said:

Ecc 1:9 The thing that hath been, it is that which shall be; and that which is done is that which shall be done: and there is no new thing under the sun.

Ecclesiastes 1:9

Solomon is confident that there is nothing new under the sun where we live including your problem.

Be confident therefore that there are more solutions to your problem than you can ever think of.

When you are hungry, look at the number of possible solutions to mitigate that problem.

Let us name a few: burgers, pizzas, rice, yam, plantain, beans, meat pie, hot dog, banana, apple and chicken.

As you can see, we can use a whole year to list solutions to this problem at hand. The solutions can overwhelm us.

Let us look at transportation. The problem of transportation is also solved in so many ways. Bicycles, trains, aeroplanes, motors, rickshaws, buses, cars and tricycles.

Here also, you can see the array of solutions. You are called to solve national problems, to solve international problems and to solve universal problems.

This means the dimensions of problems you were created to solve means that your personal problems should not overwhelm you. You must master them and attend to your real calling.

This is what have been said of you:

Mat 5:14 Ye are the light of the world. A city that is set on an hill cannot be hid.

Matthew 5:14

It is an error to halt your life because of your problems. You were born to produce solutions and the solutions lie right within you.

The problem is not intended to halt your life, it is intended to promote your life.

Too many people give excuse to why they are unable to solve problems.

Even if it will take a miracle, you must be ready to work that miracle in other to get the problem solved.

There is no scarcity of solutions in this world. There is a scarcity of men who know there are more solutions than problems.

Now, take that problem and spend time in prayer and the presence of God and begin to release the solutions that can deal with the problems that confront you so that you can go on and take on the problems of the world.

CHAPTER THIRTEEN

GOD IS ON YOUR SIDE

You are the majority if God is on your side.

From where I sit today as I write, that is the very case.

God is on your side and therefore you are the majority.

The Bible puts it beautifully:

Rom 8:31 What shall we then say to these things? If God be for us, who can be against us?

Romans 8:31

Have this consciousness as you approach life.

No matter what.

No matter what the circumstance.

Understand one truth; God is on your side.

He won't leave you, he won't forsake you. He won't let you down:

Heb 13:5 Let your conversation be without covetousness; and be content with such things as ye have: for he hath said, I will never leave thee, nor forsake thee.

Hebrews 13:5

This is the confirmation of what God intends to do by you.

To stay by you forever.

Let this confidence that God is on your side be evident in all you do.

This is what helped Joseph to live right and also to prosper.

This is what led to the success of the ministry of Jesus.

This was the testimony of Elisha when he was surrounded:

2Ki 6:16 And he answered, Fear not: for they that be with us are more than they that be with them.

2Ki 6:17 And Elisha prayed, and said, LORD, I pray thee, open his eyes, that he may see. And the LORD opened the eyes of the young man; and he saw: and, behold, the mountain was full of horses and chariots of fire round about Elisha.

2 Kings 6:16

God is on your side. His spiritual host of angels are at your disposal.

Begin to utilize hem fully.

You have more weight, more chances of victory when you begin to transact in the spirit realm.

We live in a physical world, but our battle is certainly spiritual:

2Co 10:3 For though we walk in the flesh, we do not war after the flesh:

2 Corinthians 10:3

Your time for extraordinary victory is here.

God is on your side.

Step out with boldness and take your place.

Do well to read my book on "[How to have outrageous financial abundance in no time]"

My desire is to see your progress and prosperity and freedom from negative people and circumstances. Because of that, please permit me to introduce two courses that I believe passionately will help you.

1. To cure prayerlessness, an inconsistent prayer life and the pain of not enjoying all that God has made available to you,, click [here] to learn more about my [3 Day Course] on "How to Overcome prayerlessness" that will solve the problem of prayerlessness in your life.

2. To overcome the pain of not having enough money to live where you want, eat what you want to eat and be a blessing to the multitudes around you, I have created a [7 Day Financial Abundance Course](#) that will deliver financial abundance to you quickly.

Click [here](#) to learn more about that course.

You will see increase and enlargement as you step out in faith.

FREE GIFT

Just to say Thank You for downloading my book, I'd like to give you these books for free.

Download these 4 powerful books today for free and give yourself a great future.

Click Here to Download

Your testimonies will abound. Click Here to see my other books. They have produced many testimonies and I want your testimony to be one too.

Other books by Francis Jonah

1. 3 Day Fasting Challenge: How to receive manifestation of answers

2. How to Have Outrageous Financial Abundance In No Time:Biblical Principles For Immediate And Overwhelming Financial Success

3. 5 Bible Promises, Prayers and Decrees That Will Give You The Best Year Ever: A book for Shaping Every Year Successfully plus devotional (Book Of Promises 1)

4. Influencing The Unseen Realm: How to Influence The Spirit Realm for Victory in The Physical Realm(Spiritual Success Books)

5. Prayer That Works: Taking Responsibility For Answered Prayer

6. Healing The Sick In Five Minutes: How Anyone Can Heal Any Sickness

7. The Financial Miracle Prayer

8. The Best Secret To Answered Prayer

9. The Believer's Authority (Authority Of The Believer, Power And Authority Of The Believer)

10. The Healing Miracle Prayer

11. I Shall Not Die: Secrets To Long Life And Overcoming The Fear of Death

12. Three Straightforward Steps To Outrageous Financial Abundance: Personal Finance (Finance Made Easy Book 1)

13. Prayers For Financial Miracles: And 3 Ways To Receive Answers Quickly

14. Book: 3 Point Blueprint For Building Strong Faith: Spiritual:Religious:Christian:Motivational

15. How To Stop Sinning Effortlessly

16. The Power Of Faith-Filled Words

17. All Sin Is Paid For: An Eye Opening Book

18. Be Happy Now:No More Depression

19. The Ultimate Christian: How To Win In Every Life Situation: A book full of Revelations

20. Books:How To Be Free From Sicknesses And Diseases(Divine Health): Divine Health Scriptures

21. Multiply Your Personal Income In Less Than 30 Days

22. Ultimate Method To Memorize The Bible Quickly: (How To Learn Scripture Memorization)

23. Overcoming Emotional Abuse

24. Passing Exams The Easy Way: 90% and above in exams (Learning Simplified)

25. Books:Goal Setting For Those In A Hurry To Achieve Fast

26. Do Something Lest You Do Nothing

27. Financial Freedom:My Personal Blue-Print Made Easy For Men And Women

28. Why Men Go To Hell

29. Budgeting Tools And How My Budget Makes Me More Money

30. How To Raise Capital In 72 Hours: Quickly and Effectively Raise Capital Easily in Unconventional Ways (Finance Made Easy)

31. How To Love Unconditionally

32. Financial Independence: The Simple Path I Used To Wealth

33. Finding Happiness: The Story Of John Miller: A Christian Fiction

34. Finance Made Easy (2 Book Series)

Click here to see my author page

Printed in Great Britain
by Amazon